Riding the Ripples

The Good,
The Sad
and
The Reckless

Riding the Ripples

The Good,
The Sad
and
The Reckless

Linda Hutson

PARSONS PUBLISHING

Riding the Ripples, The Good, The Sad and The Reckless
    by Linda Hutson
Copyright © 1999 Linda Hutson
All Rights Reserved.
Publisher:
    Parsons Publishing
    P.O. Box 1329
    Queen Creek, AZ 85242
    Phone: (480) 888-0141

        Publisher's Cataloging-in-Publication Data

Hutson, Linda 1954–.
Riding the Ripples, the good, the sad and the reckless /
    Linda Hutson.
        p. cm.

    ISBN: 1-928688-77-2

1. Cowboy—Poetry. 2. Ranch life—Poetry. 3. West
    (U.S.)—Poetry
    I. Title
    Library of Congress Catalog Card Number: 99-63416

        03 02 01 00 99   5 4 3 2 1

Book Design & Typesetting: SageBrush Publications, Tempe, Arizona
Jacket Design: SageBrush Publications, Phoenix, Arizona
Printing: Millennia Graphics, Colorado Springs, Colorado

Printed and bound in the United States of America

Dedication

To anyone who helped with inspiration and organisation!

Acknowledgements

Thanks to
Pete Aschenbrenner
Jack Fischer
Larry Kantor
For their photographic ingenuity!

Gwen Henson for her continuous support in organisation!

And fellow poet Jeffrey Herbert for his poem to me!!

Contents

Introduction

Riding the Ripples with Stunning Sunrise to
Beyond a Simmering Sunset

My collection of stories in various poetic forms is placed under three sections: The Good, The Sad and the Reckless. My first section commences with the sweet innocence of birth—the birth of Stunning Sunrise, on April 26, 1997, in the cool air of dawn. She was born just before the sun rose over the horizon, and an audience assembled as the light increased to watch this newborn. All of them intuitively quiet in respect of such a debut, but oh so curious at this strange little creature. What was it? Or who was it?

With the sun's first rays rose a completely formed fragile little being. Four long stick-like legs tremulously balancing this pale little body, pale as those first rays of sunlight. She instinctively gathered her uncoordinated frame to commence the first day of her life as "Stunning Sunrise." Some of my poetic stories are written through the eyes of "Sunrise" as she lived her first three months in this new found life, accompanied by photographs as evidence to the event.

From there I continue with all that I consider "good" or beautiful. Music, natural wonders, fulfillment of life, love in its simplicity, the strengths of characters in their intricacy.

"Simmering Sunset" has only recently become a part of my life; a bold little Mustang of a similar age to Sunrise. He is darker, and of course tougher, brazen but really quite shy and gentle. Forever inquisitive, but receptive to the guiding hand (nose) of his adoptive mother, Karavia.

My second section, under the title of "The Sad," looks towards the world we live in and possible reasons for sadness; perhaps lost love, broken hearts, love never found, loneliness, situations that could be considered beyond our control or unjust. Also, too briefly I talk of the animals and our surrounding environment—used and abused. Only a small collection because I like to look toward the positive.

Finally, the third section. Devious, sly, cannot be classified as "Reckless"—I use a little poetic license on this one. I write quite frequently from personal experiences—*neither* saying that I am reckless—nor the subjects. Written with a spontaneity to a particular situation, maybe sometimes a little recklessly—but not without thought!

Reflections of the Good, the Sad or the Reckless

The trio sit before me, frozen as a photograph in my thoughts.
A very pleasant picture—fit to dance the Victorian waltz?
I think not, shadows reflect every flattened flinch—
A lot is hidden within each stilted stance—

From each shadow a thousand stories could tell all—
The wizened old wizard, if he could only recall!
A measure of treasure—but so weather beaten,
Through hardship or passion, there are some mistaken!

Closer to youth, scars are better hidden—for a while—
Within the shy dimple of a smile,
Creases "of character" in time will identify themselves,
And the cruelties of life become more obvious!

From within the glint of the coyote's eye, such sly charm
    lurks—
Beauty is indeed in the eye of the beholder—so devious,
Cynicism to the satyr—
Wit of the worldly, stress for the sufferer!

Out of the three—the good, the sad or the reckless—
Who is to be the greatest?
Who the most successful?
Which is ugly—and which beautiful?

Linda Hutson

The Good

Stunning Sunrise

Sunrise—the Opening Door to Life

Under the star studded shroud of night
Was witnessed a lengthy struggle—
Beneath such a heavy blanket,
Preparation for the creation of new life—
That the gasp of that first breath should not be in vain.
That it would not shortly end in strife—
The core of life—Mother—
Suffers for the survival of them both,
She and "Stunning Sunrise"!

Each sunrise,
As the door is slowly pushed open on a new day—
Angular, shining rays of light
Creep yet again past the door of night,
Forcing those rusty hinges ajar,
Then quickly from her sight.
Encouraging a crisp clear debut to sweet innocent life!

Stunning Sunrise blossomed forth in this way—
Developing with the increasing warmth of the day,
And the nectar of her mother's milk—
She slowly strengthened to look—
Beyond eating and sleeping in her fine coat of silk,
Adapting playfully the inquisitive nature of any
    new-born babe.

Linda Hutson
Poetry Today, Wales England, G.B.
Published in Still Waters
November 1997

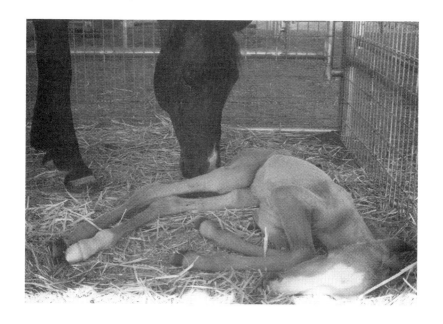

A Mother's First Born

Mother sniffing inquiringly at offspring so vulnerable,
She followed all her maternal instincts to treat her
    firstborn so caringly;
But why does the babe continue to sleep so deeply?
Even as sunshine pervades with no stealth.
They are as day and night in colour, but share a beauty of
    great wealth.
Family trait is only visible by the same white sock on the
    same fetlock.

Those dark unfocusing eyes open to gaze mistily in every
    direction.
And at last with wobbly legs she stands aching of a
    hunger so profound—
But, where oh where may that nectar of life be found?
With inherited determination so pure, nibbling in every
    quarter;
By the scent of survival contact is made as though her
    mother taught her!
As by scent, the two know they are of one!

Spindly legs strengthen to support her body beyond a
    searching stumble.
To keep those flies at bay that stumpy tail has sought
    and found its role—
How those ribs protrude so prominently from that sandy
    coloured soul!
Search again quickly to quench that sweet hungry
    tummy rumble.
Impetuously that little nose sniffs around with a
    whinnying grumble!
All it touches should turn to liquid gold in a resplendent
    warm tumble.

Mother is frustrated at not being able to take the child by
the hand—
She watches her child bodily jump in terror at any
unexpected sound,
Having been protected so long within her mother's
womb surround.
She knows well to move cautiously around her
descendant's fragility—
Lifting a rear leg enables ease of contact, with a timeless
sensitivity—
Accepting with a squeal her child's anxious searching for
sustenance.
—Life so desperate!

Linda Hutson
Quill Books
Published in Promises to Keep
October, 1997

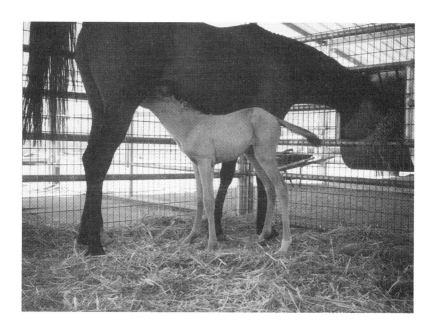

Birthday Greetings

My birthday present arrived early this year;
    not to go untold
Such a beauteous gift, no need of wrapping
    or bows to unfold
Early by a whole five days—
As all good presents should so it says!

She came into the world so quietly
    at around sunrise
Now so joyful in every new trick she tries
So golden and slight
Trembling not from her plight!

Linda Hutson

Elfin Ears

One day old
And truly fitting the mould
In texture and in profile, of a buckskin doe
Soft fine haired, in stature a little low.

Long skinny legs
Straight as a skulpted set of wooden pegs.
Tail stumpy but feathery, smokey colour clad
Wispy mane, curly and blond in strand!

But with ears turned as an elf
Hopefully magic that will not damage her health—
Accentuated by little dark tips
As the line of her lips.

Her eyes, not focusing, but so big, blue and round
Colour and lashes to astound
Wondering at the world she has found
Tail twitching with every inquisitive bound.

Linda Hutson

Troubleshooter

Today, I'm six days old
And don't like to do as I'm told!

To my own plight
I have on occasion taken flight.

Though soreness lingers little—
They still try to call me fickle.

To which I respond;
"Sunrise" is the name to which I'm bond!

Mother's always there quite close
To be certain I come to no serious throes!

Linda Hutson

All Alone

Five weeks and here I stand, alone
But without one single fear of any pursuing wrath!
Contemplating for a second my next goal
Jubilant at my stature, light footed in my path!

My ambition in life is confused;
Should I be a famous racehorse?
Can't decide—could I be a Lipizzana—
How I love to dance and prance!
Mother, in her wisdom says,
I'm a natural at taking the mountain goat stance?
Her word is to be valued, as her succulent sustenance—
In between each practice run of course!

She also tells me that one day I shall be tall and strong,
Beautiful, of course, and such a responsible, stately soul!
Quite possibly even accomplish a good motherly role—
Till then I'm just kicking up my heels—
It seems I can do no wrong!

Linda Hutson

Filly of Folly

I'm six weeks old now,
And they're enthusiastic to discipline my childish ways—
In bucking and rearing, I annoy them somehow!
So determined are they in their "training" classes!

Firstly that uncomfortable headband—they call the halter!
Then the rope with which to tie me fast—
Hindering my hiding whilst they trim my hooves
To ensure my step will never falter!

With that same rope, they coax, with pushes and shoves—
I'm no longer free to cavort, "showing off" to them all!
They're trying to convince me we're just friends,
Taking a stroll to their beck and call!

They don't like me playing at being a hoyden—
With a gentle stroking hand, and enticing words....
But with one shake of my mane at my release—
I shall show them I'm both racehorse, and foreman!

Linda Hutson

My Friend Billie

Seven weeks old, and I've found myself a friend,
Her name is Billie!
I'm so bored with the training—
She wears one collar quite simply,
Which doesn't look at all silly!
Such a lovely thing it is! In colour and in fitting!

We do have such good fun!
She loves to touch noses, and sniff around;
Only half my size maybe, but can she run!
At a great pace, she loves as I, to abound.

Obviously our curiousity to life is of equal acclaim!
She's happy at the sharp wiggling of her little tail stump
Or jumping and howling noisily!
How I wish I could do both just the same—
Strange I have no similar tricks with my rump!

I'm constantly attracted to her magical red collar—
With a big smile she'll let me nuzzle and chew,
Another item of which I have none similar—
This could be such a tasty morsel for us two!

Linda Hutson

Ponying

Their latest trick, during my eighth week of existence—
Is to take me by the halter alongside my mother!
I suppose it's quite exciting, running to keep abreast—
With someone on her back, we can move all the faster!

My only objection is the discipline—I do not wish to escape!
But with my head so firmly drawn, no room to freewheel—
And at such a pace, no time to casually survey the landscape.
I don't even get time to kick up a heel!

But really is there evidence of inability, or stupidity?
Or reason for any argument as to the luxury of life—
Mother still feeds me, and doesn't mind my trying her hay,
Perhaps I'll tow the line and enjoy life without further strife!

Linda Hutson

To Wean or Not to Wean

She was there when I awoke
But then—right after my first feed!
She was gone, as though on a puff of smoke!
They took her away with such speed.

I pleaded, I jumped and I ran with more than a prance!
I charged the gate, but she just walked on by—
Without even a backward glance;
Maybe just a little mutter, but why?

Will she come back?
Who knows, who can tell me?
Will she feed me that luscious milk for even a snack?
Questions, questions, what is it to be?

But I've found me another mate
Not my mother, he certainly can't feed me—
He'll race and jump at just the same rate.
Together we're almost the same size, as you can see!

My new mate and I share happily our hay, quite bold....
No substitute for mother's milk—a dry "acquired taste."
But isn't that life, perhaps the wisdom in growing old—
Make the best of it; wet or dry—leave no waste!

So it's weaned I be!

Linda Hutson

Simmering Sunset

This sunset simmers in a lengthy fashion
In Chino Valley
The wind gently lifts the dark mane
Of this mustang colt thereby named.

Of such simmering sorts
Generally guarding his thoughts
Until feed time that is
Then it all should be his!

Still small in size, dun in colour
But of such great valour
Brought in from the wild
While still a mere child.

Adopting quickly a new mother figure
Who accepted this role, with a soft snicker
Guiding, guarding her new child
Brought in from the wild!

Linda Hutson

Simmering Sunset
Photo by Jack Fischer

The Myth of Musical Magique

Music trickles to the ear delicately, so
Coordinating notes to words spoken so
Melodiously.

Quietly but with great strength, as
Colouring the fairytale as
Eyes glisten.

Glisten at the magique of
The rhythm spiralling within the scent of
The mystique of those deep, sweet echoes.

Echoes of age old, but timeless words.

Linda Hutson
The National Library of Poetry
Published in The Best Poems of 1998
Received Editor's Choice Award

The Tunnel to the Heart

In a vision simple, straight and wise,
The myth of life is perceived initially through the eyes.
A visual message scurried by electric energy to the soul;
Who will chase those wispy tales with passion aspark,
To roll, in colours of a rainbow,
Down the deep tearful tunnel to the heart!

Having suffered many times in timeless pre-existence,
The soul savours sentiments in no blasé fashion;
No matter the intensity, for one instant's inspiration.
Never diminishing the passion of the moment,
Exuding innocent humour—
Shining as a twinkle in the eye.
Merely watching with a gasp or a sigh!

Sad that the beauty and colour of such a vision
May sometimes be blemished by words—
Distorting a simple wondrous statement—
With verbal exaggeration—or trivialisation—
Supposedly through sophistication;
Simple words only need be used,
To capture that heart!

Perception may discern the depth to its great strength.
Reflected by those discerning beautifully shadowed,
Befringed windows of eternal wealth!
May that distant vision
Perhaps be coaxed into the tunnel to my heart!
I need say no more, just perhaps ask when it may start...
To capture my heart!

Linda Hutson

Oh, The Magique of a Tear

There is nothing more astounding than a tear;
Swelling against the eyelash.
Tremulously hanging for an instant,
Before tumbling in a tumultuous splash.
Tracing faithfully its course,
Following the force of gravity within the flow of time.

The taste of these drops of water, is sweetly salty—
As though from an ancient ocean,
Blue as the indigo orb in which our world spins—Infinity!
Encaptured from the crest of some mighty wilsome wave—
As though by magique!
Emotion overwhelming the mystique?

From this vast expanse;
Emotion catches precious droplets of windswept spray.
Accompanied by either humour or regret,
Oh tear of life, healed by a kiss?
Show me the way—
To that surrounding sea of rapturous happiness!

Linda Hutson
The National Library of Poetry
Published in A Symphony of Verse
January 1998
Received Editor's Choice Award

Gems of Eternal Strength

The Diamond;
Cut to shapely perfection
Striking life from any direction.
Hopefully catching life as light—
Joy shining in flight,
As sharply as stars in the sky at night?

The Sapphire;
So, so deep, but nonetheless bright,
Sparkling as liquid ripples without respite.
Wind on the surface of some wallowing ocean—
To such dense distance, as a mystic potion,
It ebbs and flows, can blue be so indigo?

The Pearl;
Wrenched from womb like safety—
Trapped, pierced by a clasp.
Rolled from birth in a creamy cloud so silken.
From innocence to elegance, hanging,
Hesitant in anticipation?

The Opal;
Sunlight reveals compressed liquid,
Beauty abounds, once fluid—
Between layers of chalk, streaks of colour still float!
Au naturel its heartfelt request—
Au sauvage in tranquility may it rest?

Oh which, which are you?

Linda Hutson
Iliad Literary Awards
Published in Feelings *Anthology*
November 1998
Received Honorable Mention

My Circle of Blue

Whilst I follow my twisting path, constantly
My pace is protected whilst drawn toward my destiny.
By an electric blue aura I am encircled, intensely
Blue as the indigo of Infinity.

A Raven, black with wings of a blue sheen
Hovers closeby on swirling air currents, as in a dream.
Those wings instinctively direct my trail
And I, intuitively follow his tail.

Hovering much, much closer is Tinkerbell,
Hummingbird with words of wisdom to tell—
Constantly chattering in playful whisperings
Whilst my ear echoes to the music of her wings .

You too may walk within this mirage of azure air
Where melodious colours hang to make a fairytale stir—
From the glory of infinity above
To the ocean depths never ever to dissolve.

My circle of blue is that which encircles
Us all, but I believe mine to be of an electrically strong force.
Full of glittering sparkling light, as though from sea spray,
Or the power of shooting stars on distant display.

Linda Hutson

Just Because...

Within my circle of blue;
Words whisper with the winds.
As a wave as it ripples
On the mirage which it echoes.
One that shimmers between me and you.
Oh such a hue,
Blue, in depth so true.
May you see it too!

Just because...

Linda Hutson

Fingers of Magique

The man with fingers of magique
Will release his identity and thus his soul,
Allowing freedom for his hands,
That they might dance across the strings of his guitar.
With magique gliding through melodies,
Heart rending or joyous,
It would seem haphazardly,
But finding such blissful harmony...

Either to astound or to enrapture,
Picking and strumming, always intensely,
But sometimes passionately, sometimes intricately.
As two, but with the spontaneity and fluidity of one.
The tunes as they burst or trickle forth,
Catch the hearts of any listening of any concern.
Such rest transfixed
By these vibrations of such great wealth.

No words are needed to envisage the tragedies,
Nor the serenades to such hearts.
Such fingers of magique,
In their apparition, are relentless to mesmerize—
More than just a few, with such musical dramas.
Shimmering through their souls—
Such echoes quivering on to pierce their hearts.

Inspired by magique
It seems that fingers and strings are indeed racing,
As cords run hand in hand at the speed of light,
Uniting under the direction of those fingers of magique.
This is perhaps how the sound—
Of such emotional strength is drawn forth?
It must be magique!

Linda Hutson
Favourite from Arizona's Trails of Magique *1997*

From Eternity to Infinity

Only twice a day may the Grand Canyon clefts
Into eternity, be penetrated by infinity.
Instantaneously the strobes of sun catch,
Hold and embrace the depth of their descent in stealth.
Those fingers of light delve toward the core of life

An awesome unity of the two
Reveal vivid colours of so long ago,
An intense reveling of light and matter,
To only the keen observer!
Only to be witnessed at sunset or sunrise—

Crisp stark shadows bawdily beckon the resin of light,
Seeking affection from the distant mystic blue height.
Avidly enticing the sun's rays into each frosty fissure!
Or:

Desirous of momentary rapture to lighten the dark descent,
A desperate embrace of the retreating ripples of sunlight,
Revealing its ageless voluptuous curves without repent,
Before the blanket of night, in its black mourning robe!

Joy to be taken by storm,

A musical rendering of the river, as it swells below.
The rockfaces of Eternity look toward Infinity,
To catch the liquid flow in cleansing rivulets;
Caressing crevasses borne millions of years ago!

And oh for the virginal white lacy splendour of snow!
Enrobing the rock of ages so delicately!

Linda Hutson
The National Library of Poetry
Published in Verdant Lands of Spring
Received Editor's Choice Award

Silence is Not Acquiescence

In the depth of silence
Lies great thought—
Not necessarily of acquiescence.
Affirmation is an assertive statement—
Or merely one whispered word—"Yes"!

So thereby, in my silent state
There is no reason why—
One should question the fact,
That there is any attempt to lie—
That I am not acquiescent!

And my answer is, most definitely—"No"!
From my smile—
To your sinful grin.

Linda Hutson

The Sad

Me, India 1984

Just Ripples

Full of ripples runs the river
Sometimes so clear,
From affection so near;
Nothing to fear.

Emotions show with clarity
The relevance of ecstacy
To the fullness of life
With or without strife!

but;

There are moments—when,
Angry storms rise from within.
and, ripples become frothy, frightening rapids.
Just ripples, running home—
To the mighty ocean.

So have no fear.

Linda Hutson

The Waive of a Wave

As though by majik the sway of this wave swells
Drawn by a strong appetite of deep undercurrents—
More immense than even the mightiest of oceans,
The ocean of fate is tireless!

It may plunge in one mighty surge
Shining droplets hang as they are urged—
As though by majik, backward and forward
Wherever the hunger dwells untoward—

Beckoned by wishful wishes; to create such a ripple?
Or a dream that seemed no more than fickle!
As little pebbles, we are drawn
Dredged to sand by the majik powers of this ocean!

Linda Hutson
The National Library of Poetry
To be published in The Drifting Sands, *1999*
Received Editor's Choice Award

Light Years of Love

Oh the aeons of love I hold for you!
Is it to those mystic heights that our love might rise?
Toward the dense darkness of distance!
Toward those twinkling drops of light!

—Would time allow such a continuous beauteous flight?

To swirl breathlessly on The Big Dipper by your side—
To be stabbed by such intense passion,
Inspiring a mist massive as the Milky Way—
Sensuously capturing Venus in her throbbing sway.

—Oh by a flash of lightning,
 To be transported through those light years!

Oh that you could proclaim alike by my side!
At the heavens hanging so close in their might,
With a full moon probing under the cover of night,
I stand mesmerized within the mystic circle of light.

—Any shadows of our love would be without fear of flight.

Oh peaceful as a dove I would lie with you as one!
With the moon as a window, romantically mellow,
Allowing light years to spin within its opaque glow,
Distance vanquished by such shining haze.

—So, beyond my soul's resistance!

Oh time and distance of small consequence,
I await reflection of my love to glow in your face.
Certainly with all my heart's assistance—
But where are you now, I wait on...

—Why have you gone so, so far away!

Oh that I may at least rest within your embrace;
To ponder life beneath those stars so bright,
On just one clear dark night.
Though beyond our lifetime in light years.

—Not beyond your loving arms.

Linda Hutson

Silver Blue Moon

The name "blue moon," of great eloquence—
The sky stands back in reverence
At your rare appearance
Surrounding in awe the heavens!

Hang, as you are, amongst those stars—
Please, hide not behind the clouds,
Shadowing that magical power full of pulsing dreams,
And the silvery mist, hanging as a halo, so luminous.

Solid Sea of Serenity—
Static even on that blue globe, stormy in surety,
Who stands impassive to its dominance of the night sky.
Magic of life, while we sleep, passes us by!

Tell me how I might find
One of your dreams, that it might be guided
Into my trembling hand.
Please, light my path to that end.

Linda Hutson

Life's Rainbow

My life resembles a jagged rainbow;
After each storm aplunder with
Lightning and thunder asunder
Rises life anew; in arcs of intangible colour!

Shimmering coloured streaks of light—beat with my heart,
Not blinded to the shadows of time before we part—
Nor the value of an instant within your embrace!
Before I see only the memory of your face.

May that fading distant vision be coaxed...with no strife,
To return into the vivid colours of my rainbow life
To heal the aching creases in my heart...
Now that we're apart...

I wish only one intimate, secret place—
Needing no echoes of vast empty space!
Could this not be the myth to any life,
So simple, such sweet blissful relief?

Through life's windows of love
I see the sky up above
Blue, deep, deep blue for your love.

Linda Hutson
The National Library of Poetry
Published in The Lyre's Song
November 1998

The Man Trapped in Metal

For all that time forever moves us onward,
Toward the end of the rainbow one can pray,
Hidden within, spectres of hope move us forward?
Drawn thus by fate, is it profound,
Or just the end of the day?

Whose paths shall cross, lead on this mystic flow?
More significantly than two ships passing in the night!
More impossible to know than the wonders of a rainbow?
Just hope to be in sight—
Happiness to astound is to be found.

Within the whisper that turns the heart a quiver,
Instinct follows the flow—or a "come hither"?
The smile, tremulous in it's mirth, hangs long in thought.
At the right time, in the right place, who's to know?
Heart ruling—the tracks have already been walked!

The storm blew me away,
In it's force, melodious if tempestuous—
I watch the man trapped in metal, as I float astray,
Captured as he spurs his horse
Fiercely unto the hazardous!

His posture frantic, no hill too high to climb!
Willing himself forward, toward his goal,
Heroically vital, shirt and heart aflow...
Alas, in the wrong place at the wrong time!
He will never find the end of that rainbow!

Shall I?

Linda Hutson
Favourite from Arizona's Trails of Magique *1997*

Guarded by Glass

Pressed by glass, held fast
Not one chance of advance
Nor change in expression or stance.
The quivering heart that once was,
Caught, flattened, held fast.

Untouched,
Framed by wood, to remain untouched
That beauty may last, faded, but unblemished.
A picture of beauty so innocent
To be watched, but never touched.

Once; timorous to any awhispering
Querulous at any misty breath or vibration.
Searching heavenly toward the borders of ecstacy, hovering,

Shame or even pain held no meaning.
Now guarded from even a memory of that feeling.

Linda Hutson
The National Library of Poetry
Published in Blossom in the Dawning
Spring 1999
Received Editor's Choice Award

Petals of Hope

Scented rose, pink with peace, face turned upward—
He loves me, he loves me not
Silken petals plucked
Fragrance flutters to the ground
Plucked by two fingers from a hand
To a snapping sound.

But therein is indeed some sentiment—
Hope, in pain, freedom for one second
Instead of despair at love unrequitted
Standing, wilting, wheyfaced
Fading fragrance misplaced
To crumble as dry drops of blood.

Linda Hutson
Quill Books
Published in A Time to Be Free, *1999*

The Rusty Key

Door jarred shut, the wood swollen by emotion—
Or locked as a fort against further savagery.
As a face holding within an injured heart and soul.
It can only be opened by the rusty key!

Abandoned but safely locked under that rusty key,
Without even the possibility of standing ajar.
Clambering blossom growing around to astound—
Must prove there to be at least a cringing heart!

Is this door of a face/face of a door safe from sadness?
In repelling possible pain, also the warmth of solace!
Oh the temptation of the scent of Spring's spiraling,
Chanting breeze, gently caressing the time—scarred veil,
To no avail!

Oh to be bold and devour those golden dancing rays—
Shining magic may twist into any tempting crevice!
To behind that door, persuading in swaying hypnosis.
The rusty key to catch that latch, to gasp in response—
To a smile so intense!

Trepidation at the groan of a creaking door—
Those eyes, that smile—must cross that fragile floor?
To embrace and heal a wounded, bruised heart!
Instinctively cautious, but intuitively curious,
To a serenade never stark!

Linda Hutson
The National Library of Poetry
Published in Embrace the Mornng
February 1998
Received Editor's Choice Award

Once I Was a Tree

In a wild white flash, trembling at the thunder;
I'm aghast that it should be me!
Stabbed by a fork of lightning, taken as plunder—
Why me, I'm not so bold! Nor that ugly!

Am I to be split in two—untoward!
Or shall I survive, with merely a distorted stiff limb?
Locked in my frame, pointing an accusatory arm skyward!
I am tied to my roots, how may I avoid the shame?

If pain I must suffer, may the end be short if not sweet!
By this sudden jagged terminal stab—I am happy to die—
That my ashes may fertilize the land after the lapse of heat!
My soul stands awaiting, that my spirit might be free to fly!

Often, I have watched jealously as the birds flutter freely,
Rising on the transparent currents of air unto the sky,
Beyond any traumas entrapped in this world. So simply—
If this is to be the end, may I not just fly?

I prefer any death more brief than that hack of an axe.
What sin have I committed—to be cut-down as firewood,
Or become pieces of some jigsaw puzzle house box—
Torn limb from limb, living flesh, is it not understood?

Imagine, the circling, grinding of an electric saw.
To my final shriek and one last shudder, such I would fall.
Jagged metallic teeth bite inch after inch, all blood and gore!
Deaf to the flailing, rustling of dying leaves as they call!

In pursuance of the true cycle of life, I carry my fruit!
Man continues selfishly to use and abuse—
The air and water essential to existence, they pollute!
Can we ever work with life under such a self-indulgent ruse?

Habitation blindly is his comfort,
—Without any sensitivity toward the environ!
May humanity be humble to the fragility of this beauteous
—Spinning sphere!
Felling forests so freely,
—They are crucifying us all within their pavilion!
Possibly without even the ritual of a wooden cross to bear!

Linda Hutson
Quill Books
Published in Promises to Keep
February 1998

Irony of Ironwood

A tree so strong, as aged iron, blackened
By life, cruelly stiffened and distorted.
With springtime, fluttering young leaves
That rustle so happily in the breeze,
Cosset protectively the fragile blossoms,
Flirtatiously pink and sweet as candyfloss.
Tickling that visually dead tree, so old and grey.
Could they not turn its heart astray?

TWO HEARTS AS ONE?

My heart was yours, I told you so.
In wooden words
You spoke of sweetness and light,
Of how perhaps one day you might
Allow your heart to be mine,
A combination so fine.
To be, or not to be real,
We'll see, as we feel.
If, when, and how it should be?
Springtime, hopefully!

Linda Hutson

Wolf in the Wilderness

Wild wolf in the snow, head pointed upward,
—Standing stiff and bold.
Howling in happiness I hope!
Substantially dressed against this blizzard
—In a beautiful grey coat!
Oh but his feet must be so, so cold.

—Certainly, joy or sadness, he should not be standing alone!

The snowflakes fall thick and fast,
—Blown into feathery drifts.
Perhaps he is disorientated, a lost scout?
If not for the windblown snow,
—Surely by scent he would have found the route.
Perhaps an outcast, crying in despair.

—No pack to track his prints!

The question is wit against skill—feeble fails!
Wolves survive in forest shadow or snowy prairie.
Humanity considered them such a life threat;
To barbarically obtain that lusty, beautiful pelt!
It has become habitual—
For the animal to use its virtual invisibility.

—Changing as a chameleon to the season's colours!

continued

Need for food is undeniable, no one's arguing that!
Such a pitiful presence put forth by the coyote,
A cousin to the wily wolf—
But rarely with such a sleek, fine coat;
A scavenging coward, more like a rat!
Partly domesticated—whose fault is that!

—Skulking in the sunset,
Any creature must be considered both woe, and prey.

Linda Hutson
The National Library of Poetry
Published in The Best Poems of 1997
Received Editor's Choice Award

Searching Invisibility

(True Story)

I gaze with twitching ears at this disturbingly noisy foe.
I stand as a statue of stone, that I might merge with the
    flickering light,
I would like to be unseen—but can I sink that low?
Heart thumping, I watch with unblinking eyes, ready to
    take flight.

The sweet moist odour tickles my nose telling me water
    is near—
These sultry shadows are respite from the desert's deadly heat;
This heat rippling upward, obscures the opacity of my fear!
I'm so weary and I wish only to rest a little, while I eat.

Oh that I might peacably be allowed also to quench my thirst.
Briefly before the sun disappears from sight—
With the stars, four legged whining woes follow the scent
    with which I'm cursed—
Peace to all man, I'm not looking for a fight!

Linda Hutson
The National Library of Poetry
Published in A Painted Garden
October 1997
Received Editor's Choice Award

Hands of Majik

(True Story)

Just as the fairy Tinkerbell, sparkling in the sun,
Ashimmer in the mist of magique.
Flirting in an air show, too high, too flighty.

From impact, gravity proved this weightless waft—
To be not from a fairytale.
Rescued within the palm of my hand.

Miniscule! Beak ajar, gasping for breath.
Paralyzed by all but her pounding heart,
And those little black eyes blinking.

Several minutes passed!

Sugared nectar suckled from my fingertip—
Energy flowed from within, sufficient to stir.
Balancing on those tiny feet, with no harm done?

Both of us anxious, I opened my hand.
Both wings as a butterfly fluttered,
But although impatient, still too weak—

Again trusting my soft grasp.
Oh to recreate the fairy named Tinkerbell
That she might fly once more!

Oh my healing hand.

Linda Hutson
The National Library of Poetry
Published in A Picture of Elegance
March 1998
Received Editor's Choice Award

The Feat of Fate

Just one second, one gasping phrase
Could change the lengthy circles
Of your little world
Into a spiralling whirl!

Be it a word from your mouth
Or step, east, west, north or south
One stride in the wrong direction—
And you may forever be thinking—

Could it have been me,
Should it have been me?
Maybe it could still be me!
Will it ever be me?

Just recall
Those fateful steps as they fall,
And, please oh please
Don't say—*jamais de la vie*!

Linda Hutson
The National Library of Poets
Received Editor's Choice Award
To be published in Hearts of Glass
and A Celebration of Poets

Au Revoir

Time, oh what a time
Time to say with a sigh
goodbye.
Why, why oh why
You ask me why
I'm such a nice guy.

Where, where should I go
Where will your image not follow me so
Where might I go?
How much time, how much pain
Wandering without aim
In fear of seeing your face again.

When oh when will it be
That I shall be free to see
How it should be?

With me? *Jamais de la vie!*

Linda Hutson
The National Library of Poetry
To be published in Captured Moments
February 1999
Received Editor's Choice Award

Ecstatic Effervescence

I gaze into the shapely bluey green bottle;
Champagne is her name;
Contemplating as I am, in solitude—
We must both feel nostalgia at the loss of
Such flavourful effervescence.
Having been consumed, enjoyed—
We both stand empty,
Containing merely deep, dark shadows—
As though abandoned, null and void!

An intense beauteous bottle,
Standing proudly—clothed with a label of some repute.
Sadly mourning the loss of the frothy liquid energy
She had once guarded. This liquid had run,
Expounding profusely its bubbly worth,
Pursuing explosion of the cork—
Resembling in strength,
A great escape from lifelong imprisonment.
"Ecstatic effervescence"—so impatient to witness
The long stemmed grace of that glinting glass goblet!

For myself,
That hollow tinted body still contains
A scented aromatic air of circumstance.
It is impossible to diminish the power
Of a memory thus sustained;
Even though in reality "ecstatic effervescence"
Is a passing magique so brief—
No box, bottle or casing may suppress
This fountain of mirth! Such a power,
Colouring life as the touch of a wisping hand.

This bottle shall be filled with blue flowers,
Echoing that shaded, yet glistening glass.
As ornamentation,
Sometimes they will surely catch my eye—
And my heart, for a several seconds.
Perhaps in a wish to draw down and embrace
That delicate aura; so tremulous!
That memories may remain as the magic of the moment?
Just as the encircling charisma released from
"Ecstatic effervescence"!

Linda Hutson
The National Library of Poetry
Published in The Scenic Route
May 1997
Received Editor's Choice Award

Forever

You talked of loving me—forever

That you would protect me—forever

But you lied...

You will be but a haunting shadow—forever

A ghostly figure caught at a glance—forever

A soft whisper in my dreams—forever

Will you even remember me—Ever?

Linda Hutson
Sparrowgrass Poetry Forum
To be published in Poetic Voices of America
March 1999

The Reckless

Me, Australia 1985

Warbling Wonderdog Nellie

(True Story)

Once I had four legs—but then I lost one!
It seems difficult to recall—ever having more fun—
Or a time when I ever possessed more than Three!
Look at the smile on my face and you could only agree!

I've less trouble with less legs to clean,
Less legs on which to catch so many cactus spear,
My tail now assumes the role of "balancer" in rockclimbing!
Even though, if need be, my tail wags with forceful feeling!

I still chase rabbits, lizards and birds with spirit,
My bark is a guard that tells intruders to run at a sprint!
I'll playfully cajole the burro,
But to avoid his kicking hoof, I'm not slow!

Solitary rear limb does more work than play—
But with endeavour, grows stronger each day.
Sometimes I'm called the mischievious black eyed wonder!
Other times; "Long Tongue"—dependant upon my candour—

But if you see me from the right profile—
You'd know no better than I!
Three legs or four—sunshine glistening on my coat;
I move too fast to keep count!

Just to show I've a keen ear, on occasion,
I'll catch the tune of a fellow artisan
And happily participate with my own rendering;
Anything from delicate tinkling tones; to a hearty howling!

Linda Hutson

Billie Don't Tell Nellie

Billie please don't tell Nellie—
She just wouldn't understand.
Not even a whisper Billie,
She'd catch any word that got around.

Just one word about Perky Percy—
And she'd recall, she'd be jealous.
Just because I played with Percy!
So not one sound—our little secret, Please!

She knows what fun is to be found—
Fooling with Perky Percy, its true.
But with a promise I say to you now;
Harmless it was; I'd not lie to you!

Just full of laughter and games—
But Nellie's revenge would not be sweet,
So to speak, she has sharp teeth
With which to rent her wrath!

So Billie, please, please don't tell Nellie...

Linda Hutson

Legend of the Round Table

(True Story)

From the chasms of the mineshaft
Echoes on the electric wires waft
Of the voices to be heard but never seen?
Of Dave and Bob's piercing tones so keen!!

Their opinions or comment,
To news worthy of torment!
Such scepticism, such wit!
From such as they sit!

They battle as would knights at the round table
With words of scorn, not silver swords of the fable.
Neither are they clad in protective attire
To not one suit of armour do they aspire!
Perhaps they should!

Their surround is indeed a panorama,
Seated upon a platform, as any good drama—
Encircled by the wisdom of our century,
Under the title technology
Quotations flutter from each and every anthology.

They fight over and along sparks of electricity,
With a cackle of mirth to any adversity.
Words fly as doves across this table—
Or as bullets from a gun; Tis but a friendly battle!

Linda Hutson

Sunny Spring Sunday

(True Story)

Ushered by echoes of music, I wandered
    wistfully into the oasis!
Soft, magically cool air swayed through
    my hair and across my face.
I was instantly hypnotised by the rousing
    rhythm, and the dancers
Wrapped in sundrenched colours stolen
    from springtime flowers!

Who, playful with the flamenco music,
    arched spine to flexing shoulders—
To the pleasure of glistening sun, flinging
    arms to grasping fingertips—
Guitar, flute and drums coercing with
    mesmerizing melodies—
And howls of pleasure at the stamping of
    feet and pulsing castanets!

Those throbbing, dancing shoes hit the
    ground so emphatically,
As fleeting feathers blown by the wind
    visually.
Abrupt tilt of a chin to the sharp tap of a
    heel—a proud profile of beauty—
Flirting breeze, turning flouncing skirts to
    clouds floating iridescently!

The vivid strumming of fingers to the
    instrument of each musician—
Spirals of music amongst the aromas of
    fragrant spices—such a creation,
To an audience compelled to shout or clap
    in passion—
To chords of music circled by flighty
    hummingbirds diving in unison!

Linda Hutson

Shadow of a Vampire

What do you see from those deep caves
you've got there?
Your life trapped in those shadows is
indeed a cross to bear—I know though,
through sound of great splendour you've won your glory—
But is it selfless sensitivity you're searching?
This can only be a sad story!

Within that shadow lies such a powerful face;
But should I take your words as true,
Or merely farce?
I wonder, more than you,
At what I hear but cannot see written before me—
At the spoken word of such a man,
That you are, will be, want to be!

There is light within that darkness—
I'm sure this to be so;
But perhaps,
Only when the sun is very, very low—
Drawing for an instant on a heart filled
with pulsing happiness,
Leaving behind bleeding, jagged chasms of
such great emptiness!

May your success bring you happiness,
But it is known—
As penance, a great pain may be borne.
Similar to bright light after the darkness of
a starless night—
Take care,
One with such "light" sensitive sight.

I know now my words previously put
forth to be true.
So who am I to rue!
And not to sound like any old cynic—
I've descended with the Titanic!

Linda Hutson

Viper or Vampire?

Hypnotised to the point of paralysis
By the flashing swirling depths of those eyes
Coerced into oblivion by the soft whisper
From the sensuous smile which rises to a lazy leer.

Thus, the rebirth of the vampire
Encircling submissive soul as a viper
Drawn toward the softest flesh to be torn
Fangs delve deep, pain neverending to be borne.

Thunder will echo forever around the jagged caverns
Created by those lightning white, impatient fangs
The devouring fangs of fate
Carried by this creature who will never wait!

In wielding this ravage
Leaving a red river of forever pulsing pillage
The myth is true, such wounds are never to heal.
Such is fate, or fortune, who could reveal?

Linda Hutson
The National Library of Poetry
Published in Outstanding Poets of 1998
Received Editor's Choice Award

Naked to Time

Naked in both the physical and emotional.
In truth not alone, but two as one—.
Two within the sensuary treasure of touch,
Cavorting, caressing in chase of ecstacy.

To mean so little, or so much,
Wishfully wallowing in search of affection?
Such, together within blissful harmony—
Fulfilling at the very least links of the body.

In such unity, passions aspark,
Such great strength may last but a few moments—
In this lapse of time no lies may hide
within those folds of flesh,
Chasing those wispy tales tremulously to the heart.

Desperate to come to no grief!

Just remember—
I'm deep, physically, and emotionally—
Beware of falling into such a swirling spiral,
You could be plunged into the chasms of my heart.

Linda Hutson
The National Library of Poetry
Published in A Pleasant Reverie
August 1998
Received Editor's Choice Award

From Hirt to Hurt

Of the cowboy Hirt I am a fan
He is indeed the "stetson man"
Not hurt at all
He stands good and tall.

From that bushy moustache echoes a drawl
In a "camera proud" surly scowl
Which can tilt to a mirthful grin
Should there be any hearts to win!

Not just your average cowboy
Only in true "hats of the west" does he have time to toy...
A "custom made" hat man, is he
I just want to know where is the one he's promised me!

Linda Hutson

Photo by Larry Kantor

The Race

The Race, The Pace,
The Race of Life!
Love and joy, won with ease,
With hopefully little loss of face.

But could this not be boring,
No excitement, no flow of adrenaline.
No sadness means no glory,
No content to the story!

To laugh, sing, or cry—
Whatever the reason why?
Good, bad, sad or reckless,
Such release is relief of stress.

Oh for a little grace to this race!

Linda Hutson
Iliad Press
Published in Crossroads *October 1998*
Received Honorable Mention
1999 President's Recognition for Literary Excellence
Sponsored by The National Authors Registry

The Wanton Waiter

With not one hair on his frame
They call him a model,
No clothes to question his claim to fame.
Physically immobile—
He is painted, standing, cheekbones held high.
No wayward glance,
Nor change of body stance,
Only thoughts may spiral as they dance.

This naked man—
Proud, but modest as he poses.
Simplistically, muscularly strong—
Smooth lines for budding artists—
To create an impressive vision.
A futuristic, male Mona Lisa? Perhaps!
Bald, but Statuesque!
Is it all down to chance?

Linda Hutson

The Sheriff's Worth Is Never Done

Oh, Mr Sheriff, Sir, please let me take your name—
Your eyes hide behind those glasses so shyly,
You most surely would be of instant stately fame—
Especially if I named you in my story!

This story is related in grand furore...
As the I.17 weaves onto the I.10 in construction—
Connected by coloured cones by the score...
Traffic trailing in multiple lines of progression!

These lines followed numerous a diversion—
Rapidly reducing speed limits from 75-55-35-
Danger indeed and creation of total confusion!
There was little chance of speedy brake reaction!

Behind your glasses all must have passed in a blur—
Until that all too distinctive blue flash of a Bronco—
I was innocently following the flow Sir, no more!
Exceeding the limit a trifle, but then weren't we all?

Your values I've no wish to slur, Sir!
You have my sympathy; all I ask, Mr Sheriff, Sir,
Is that perhaps you be a little more friendly, Sir—
Not so blinded by your duty, Sir!

Citation, right or wrong, you're the law,
Was I really racing the pace you cited me for?
Who's to argue, question, what, why, wherefore?
Gulp—perhaps I should claim anonymity also?

Linda Hutson

Just a Dream

The cowboy tipped his hat and said hi
As he jauntily swaggered by.
Such a cheeky grin, with the wink of an eye—
Hinting possible cheeky sin, with not even a sigh!

Oh dream of mine...

In a dream of mine! it might just have been—
That handsome cowboy I'd just seen.
If he hadn't straddled his mount, turned in a dusty spin,
And chuckled, as he galloped toward the sinking sun!

Oh dream of mine...

The Cowboy who tipped his hat, oh but why...
Did he never say goodbye...
He could have grasped me oh so close, in that dusty spin—
And danced as a dark silhouette, to beyond that sinking sun.

Oh dream of mine...
Following that sinking sun!

Linda Hutson

Friend or Foe?

So many times in retrospect I've instinctively felt,
I should not have done that!
But living is not only by my own *faux pas*,
But with those also of others!

Friends and foe alike!

Dismissing with a chuckle—wherever unharmful,
Adapting to, sympathizing with the soulful—
Helping ease the pain, or the shame...
That they should do the same?

A quick shrug; puts it all down to experience!

How can we ever be so vain.
When it should be so plain?
With our supposedly superior
Savior! 'Tis often blunder put asunder!

All from those narrow corridors of the brain—

Following the bad—
There must follow the good...
Willpower and patience together,
Such strength! Oh that such could last forever...

So value every second of those magical time lapses!

Linda Hutson
Poetry Guild
Published in A Celebration of Poets, *October 1998*

The Jump of a Lifetime

(True Story)

—Just one dark evening I found the true
rhythm within my stride—
Under such a warm, star filled sky,
I was tardy in my chores.
So determined was my stride,
that nothing dare hinder the pace—
So guilty was I to speedily deliver hay to
hungry neighs!
And hence return to the comfort of
shadow free floors!

—Reason for delay in fulfillment of evening duties...
Perhaps 'twas the wine by which my race
was thus accelerated!
Socialising with new found friends,
jovial jargon; way past sunset!
Distance blurred as I flew
on legs stretched to a bounding glide—
Leaped clear of patio,
flicking electric light switch enroute.

—That my step was thus stretched, was very
lucky!
Shout from behind—
"you just jumped over a rattler"!
One glimpse was enough,
witnessing indeed an angry prattler!
My forward projection
most definitely did not lapse!
So intent upon reaching my goal—
hay for the whinnying nags—

—I'm certain the wine dispelled even a flicker of my
concentration—
That snake was looking for a fight,
not merely parading his stance!
But not a fool,
he acknowledged my vitesse to be no prance—
Courage also,
because he stood to attention, aggressively—
But happily, decided it was preferable
to retreat graciously.

—Thus he delved, undefeated, idly dawdling,
into the darkness!

Linda Hutson

Stunk Out the Skunk

(True Story)

Could it have been a mouse?
Creeping noisily under my house—
But more likely a stealthy rat
Determined to get fat!

Verbal advice however
Advised the mammal more likely than never
To be a slinky skunk
A lot of spunk, but it never stunk!

Following this advice to change his home
Not tempting, like a dog to a bone
Truly, like a moth to a mothball
This stripey little scratcher didn't like them at all.

So instead of the stench of skunk trails
Within my house hung the vapour of mothballs
So I shall have no moths in my clothes,
But, Chino please blow a gale through my windows!

I've had enough now... My sinuses are clear!

Linda Hutson

Words of Parting

If I sing this song my friend,
The story's all for you,
So if one day we meet again,
The story must be true.

It's such a pretty story,
In words seldom led astray;
Held captive not for glory;
So don't let them run away.

Seize my words gently,
In a soft and tranquil place;
That they might whisper shyly—
The secrets of my solitary space.

The sun's rays will warm the soul—
Could my song encircle your heart so?
My words are searching as an aureole—
That they may make your heart glow!

But keep waiting... I've still to sing!

Linda Hutson
Favourite from Arizona's Trails of Magique *1997*
Also recorded by Hilltop Records in 1998

To Linda

The magic of your flowing hair, tempered by the sun,
A heart that has a pounding sound.
And a repeated strong refrain
That almost knocks me off the ground,
"Hark," I can hear it now, and yet again.
Tremor of it awakes my thoughts,
Of you and your glowing smile.
For each day I will remember
That very day that I met you.
The day is nigh, and we must go,
Returning yet another day,
The sky has darkened and the sun is low,
Has put an end in a perfect way.

Written for me by: Jeffrey E. Herbert

Honorably Onerous

She wasn't born with it—
She earned it.
She calls it wit!

They call it aggressive,
At best assertive.
Admittedly never passive!

Never meaningfully malicious.
Unintentionally onerous, perhaps—
Wistfully turning toward humorous!

On occasion wishful—
In wile immeasurable,
In affection unquestionable!

I know only 'tis I
My words just won't whisper by
I know not why!

An unintentional onerary
In no way ordinary
So it just must be honorary!

Linda Hutson

Photo by Pere Aschenbrenner

About the Author

Three years ago I followed my heart to Arizona. (It was at this time that my writing truly commenced.) Prior to this my home was England, the country in which I was born. My career as a bi-lingual sec./P.A. (French being my second language) lasted approximately fifteen years working in the centre of London with several American companies. However my love was to travel, and I did spend a couple of years in both France and Norway, and travelled extensively spasmodically. During this time, I had no thoughts of writing (or time). I was either socialising, travelling, cleaning up after myself, or working, (saving for my next trip).

Having found Arizona, my initial poems were to be songs to accompany, perhaps accelerate, my progress in learning to play the guitar. So briefly I have been classified as a "cowgirl poet." I was then encouraged to enter several pieces of work into various competitions, and from there to publishing my first anthology *Arizona's Trails of Magique*. Since then the guitar hasn't received all the attention it should.

Arizona opened its doors to my imagination, and became my inspiration. I ride my horses almost every day, and I continue to be amazed at the beauty of the countryside. Incredible indigo blue skies and vast vistas of glorious space. Breathtaking extremes—desert, with massive ravines and pillar rock formations, to pine forests and snow capped mountains. The Taj Mahal and Ayers Rock, seen whilst travelling, have been dwarfed by Arizona.

Whilst drawn into the complexities/frustrations of writing/publishing my poetry, I have become a member of various literary organisations: The Arizona Book Publishing Association, The Arizona Poets Society, the National Library of Poetry and the International Society of Poets, from whom I have received many "Editors Choice Awards," and the "International Poet of Merit Award." Iliad Press, having awarded me several "Honorable Mentions," have most recently awarded me the distinction of excellence in the 1999 President's Recognition of Literary Excellence, sponsored by The National Authors Registry. It is they who recommended me to the National Authors Registry, hence I am now a registered author! The Poetry Guild, Quill Books and Sparrowgrass Poetry Forum are each publishing pieces of my work.

In July of 1998, I transferred myself, horses and hounddogs north of Phoenix for a short spell (nine months), never leaving Arizona, but searching out the cool breezes of Chino! During my stay, I joined the Professional Writers of Prescott Club and also the Artists Club. It is from Chino that I coordinated the publication of this, my second anthology, *Riding the Ripples, the Good, the Sad and the Reckless*! Thereafter, I've promised my guitar a little more time, and a more concentrated effort, having moved back south to the sun!

Finally, even though my loves and losses are as you read, my concern for the elephant is never ending. In my first anthology—*Arizona's Trails of Magique*, this is very apparent, poetically. This time I have limited myself to several personal photographic visions, depicting all three: the Good, the Sad and the Reckless!

Linda Hutson

Order Form

☐ Yes! Please send me *Riding the Ripples* plus these other titles
by Linda Hutson.

Name ....
Address ....
City ....State...........................Zip......
Phone ....Fax...

Book Title	Qty.	Cost Ea.	Total
Riding the Ripples, The Good, *The Sad and The Reckless* (hardcover)	_____	$16.95	_____
Arizona Trails of Magique (softcover)	_____	$ 9.95	_____

	Sub-total	$_____
Arizona residents add 7.4%	Tax	$_____
$3.20 per book	Shipping	$_____
	TOTAL	$_____

Mail order and make check payable to:
  Parsons Publishing
  P.O. Box 1329
  Queen Creek, AZ 85242–1329

American Express, Visa and MasterCard accepted

Card # _____Exp date _____ /_____

To order by phone call 1-480-888-0141.